STEPHEN'S HISTORY OF SAINTS

STEPHEN

· ILLVSTRATED BY ·
STEPHEN PEPLER · AGED 6
· WRITTEN BY ·
LOTTIE HOARE

CARDOZO KINDERSLEY · CAMBRIDGE 1992

St. Patrick 390 – 461 AD

When St. Patrick was a little boy he was not a saint at all.
In fact he was not very interested in being a Christian
and nor did he pay any attention to his teachers. He
came from a village called Bannaven Taberniae. This
village was somewhere on the west coast of England but
no one can work out where it is now because it was
destroyed and other villages with different names grew
up in its place. One day when Patrick was out playing on
the beach, he was snatched by Irish pirates and carried
away across the seas to be sold as a slave in Ireland.

SP ATRICK
MADE A SLAVE

When Patrick got to Ireland he had to tend sheep on a hillside for six years. As he spent lots of time by himself he started to pray. He then decided that praying was rather good for him and he would say as many as one hundred prayers in a single day – and almost as many in the night. One day Patrick heard a voice saying 'You will go to your own country, see your ship is ready'. Patrick set off straight away and travelled 200 miles until he found his ship. He then set sail and when he reached England he travelled through deserted countryside for 28 days feeling particularly hungry until, after a great deal of praying, he found some wild honey. When he reached his home village again his family helped him train to be a priest and when he had finished his training he travelled back to Ireland and taught the Irish about Jesus. Patrick realized that if you converted the chiefs of the tribes to Christianity then they would convert their tribesmen and save him a lot of work. Patrick could also work miracles. Some people believe that he banished snakes from Ireland and others that he could travel across the seas from Rome to Ireland, sitting on the top of a floating rock. He could also turn a man into a wolf and light a fire with icicles. When St. Patrick died there was no night time for nearly two weeks.

The Shamrock leaf which is the national Irish symbol, was thought to be able to protect you from witches, terrible powers and from wailing banshees if you were wandering across lonely moors. If you picked a Shamrock leaf while you were wearing gloves it was supposed to make an ill person well again.

HE MINDS SHEEP

Columba 521 – 597 AD

No one knows exactly why Columba left Ireland (Erin) in the year 563 and set sail for Iona. Some said it was because of an argument between monasteries. One group of monks claimed that another group of monks had stolen a holy book. Perhaps he was fed up with all this arguing and wanted some peace and quiet. He set up a monastery on Iona and taught the Picts about Christianity.

Columba did such a lot of praying that he too could work miracles. He could predict when sea monsters would loom up from under the waves; he knew what spelling mistakes the monks had made in their books without even reading them; he could predict that a man was going to let a book drop into the water, that another was about to spill ink; he could make bitter fruit sweet and increase a small herd of cattle from five to one hundred and five; and he could expel demons who lurked in cups of milk. This particular miracle was rather messy because the demon would panic when he popped his head up from under the milk and caught sight of Columba and then the demon would leap out of the cup sending milk splattering everywhere; but when Columba blessed the cup it became full to the brim again.

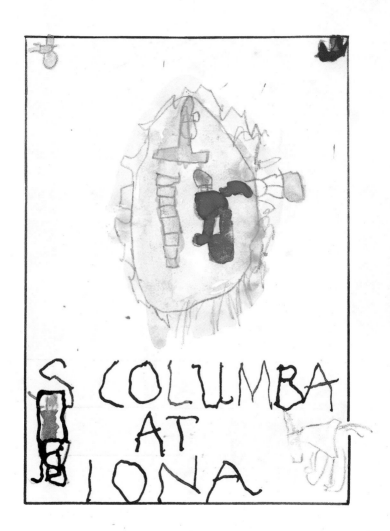

COLUMBA
AT
IONA

Gregory the Great 540 – 604 AD

Although many people in Iona in the North of England had heard about Jesus at this time, because people like Columba had sailed across from Ireland to let them know, the people in the South of England had not yet met many Christians. But this was to change, after a man called Gregory took a walk in Rome. Gregory was wandering through the bustling market place when he caught sight of some children being sold as slaves. They had fair complexions, fine features, and thick golden hair. Gregory asked the man who was selling them what country the children were from and what was the name of the people there. He was told that they came from Britain and that the people there were known as Angles. 'Not Angles but Angels!' cried Gregory 'For that is what they look like with their golden hair.' Gregory thought it was a shame that people who looked so much like angels had not yet heard about Jesus or anything to do with angels. So, when he became Pope he sent St. Augustine and his monks off to the south of England to teach the Angles to be Christians.

ENGLISH

SEVALS

CHILDRENSOLDAS

Saint Augustine DIED 604 AD
King Ethelbert 560 – 616 AD

The first time Augustine and his monks set out on their journey from Rome to England they panicked and fled back homewards again. They were very worried because they had heard frightening stories about how the Angles were all fierce-looking pagans who were looking forward to chopping Christians up into tiny pieces. Gregory told them very kindly but firmly that they must be brave and they must get on with their job. Augustine and his monks set out for England again still with giddy feelings in their stomachs, which were made worse by the fact that they had to swish about on the high seas for a good while until eventually they reached Kent. Ethelbert, king of Kent, heard of their arrival and he was very curious about these men from Rome.

Ethelbert's wife Bertha was already a Christian because she had learned about Jesus when she had lived in France before she was married. Ethelbert, though, was very fond of the pagan gods that he had known about since he was a small boy and he did not want to change his religion. You might think that the pair of them would argue about this matter, but as it turned out Ethelbert was a kindly sort of chap and he liked to see Bertha cheerful. He thought that Christians ought to do their own thing and he should do his without them getting on each other's nerves. Ethelbert suggested to St. Augustine and his monks that they all meet up on the small island of Thanet. You can see their meeting in the picture. Bertha is standing behind Ethelbert and she is wearing a little crown.

KING ETHELB ERT

S. AUGUSTINE

Ethelbert was friendly to Augustine and his men but he was a bit worried by all these stories of miracles that he had heard. That was why he decided it would be better to meet Augustine and his men out of doors so that he could easily run away if they started to do anything extraordinary. He could not understand how miracles worked so he was afraid of them. All the same, he gave Augustine and his monks a house in Canterbury and enough land on which to build two churches. St. Augustine and his monks carried a big brown board with Jesus painted on it. This board had travelled all the way from Rome with them and in fact it probably would have had very fine decoration on it in rich colours like red and gold. St. Augustine and the monks would enter each town carrying a silver cross as well as this board and they would sing as they walked. The people of Kent had never seen such things before. Soon large numbers of people in Kent became Christians and eventually Ethelbert, realizing that this was the religion his people had chosen, became a Christian too. Pope Gregory was very pleased about this and sent King Ethelbert a letter and some little presents.

S. AUGUSTINE

St. Aidan DIED 651 & St. Oswald DIED 642 (A Royal Saint)

King Oswald of Northumbria gave Aidan the island of Lindisfarne so that he could build a monastery. Aidan became the first Abbot there. Aidan did not think it was a good thing to have lots of belongings and fancy clothes. Once he was given a fine horse but he gave it away to a poor man. He did not like to ride a horse when he went into the villages to talk to the people because he thought it made him look too important. Aidan did not like boasting and he and his followers lived as they taught. That is to say they did not tell people they must eat dry bread and then go and stuff themselves full of cake. They would eat dry bread too. Aidan used the money that wealthy men gave him to pay the ransom in order to get slave boys free. He then taught them reading and writing and how to become bishops. In those days learning to read and write was almost always connected with the church because there were not many books made then except religious ones. When Penda the pagan king of Mercia tried to burn the town of Bebba, Aidan prayed for the wind to change and it did. The flames blew back and burnt Penda's men instead. Aidan was leaning on a buttress in a church when he died and when Penda later burnt down the church the buttress would not burn. The flames licked through the very nail holes by which the buttress was attached to the building but still the buttress did not burn down.

Oswald was a Christian king and early in his reign he sent for a bishop to preach to his men to try and make them become Christians. The first bishop who arrived was bossy and rather snooty about Oswald's men, thinking they were wild and ignorant because they did not know about Jesus yet. This bishop went home to Iona grumpily and declared that these Northumbrian men were too difficult to teach. Next bishop Aidan arrived who was much more gentle and not in such a hurry. He knew Oswald's men were not all going to be Christians by the end of the week.

Oswald liked listening to Aidan's wise words and one evening he invited Aidan to supper. A great silver dish full of delicious food was placed on the table in front of them. Just as they were about to start eating someone whispered in Oswald's ear that there was a crowd of hungry people in the road outside who were crying out for food. Oswald ordered that the delicious food that he and Aidan were about to eat should be taken away and given to the crowd, and that the great silver dish should be smashed up and small pieces of silver handed out to the poor. You can see this meal going on in the picture with the hungry crowd waiting and the Angels at the top of the page reminding Aidan and Oswald of what it is only fair to do.

AIDANAN O SWALD

Oswald was a king who kept losing his kingdom. First of
all he lost it to Edwin, and then when he had won it back
Oswald was killed by Penda in the battle of Masefield.
Oswald's body was cut into pieces by Penda's men. The
head, arms and hands were hung up on stakes. Monks
later collected the bits of Oswald's body and believed

KING PENDA KILLS OSWALD

that if ill people touched them then they would be cured of their illnesses. Several people claimed to have Oswald's head so after a while nobody knew which head really had been Oswald's. Poor Oswald could not be made well again, though some said that Oswald's hands would never rot because they had been so generous when he was alive.

St. Hilda DIED 680 AD

When Hilda was a new born baby, Hilda's mother was feeling very miserable, for, although she had a new daughter someone had just poisoned her husband. All of a sudden Hilda's mother felt something odd under her dress. 'Hmmm!' she thought to herself and when she undid the brooches on her dress she discovered she was wearing a fine necklace that shone so brightly that it lit up the whole of Britain. This necklace was a sign from God that baby Hilda was going to grow up to do great things. When Hilda did grow up King Oswy asked her if she would look after his baby daughter and in return he would give Hilda enough land for ten families. On this land Hilda built the Abbey of Whitby which became famous for its learning. Kings, rulers and ordinary people all came and asked Hilda's advice when they had problems. Hilda did not like wars and she thought that everyone should share all their belongings; then they would not need to fight and no one would be poor and needy. All Hilda's friends called her 'mother', because although she did not have any children of her own, living in her abbey was like living in a great big family. Of course the nuns and monks there sometimes squabbled just like brothers and sisters do. Hilda was very ill for the last six years of her life but she still struggled on, and wobbled around her abbey on her spindly old legs trying to get all the work done that needed to be done.
In the end Hilda was attacked by a particularly nasty fever and she died in the morning when the cock crowed.

A nun called Begu saw a vision that the roof had been lifted off so that Hilda could be carried up to heaven by angels. Before people understood about fossils they thought that the ammonites in the rocks around Whitby were snakes beheaded and turned into stone by the prayers of St Hilda.

Caedmon DIED 680 AD

Caedmon could not sing at all, in fact he could only croak. He dreaded going to parties where people might ask him to sing and when they did he would make excuses that he had to get back and look after his cows and he would go off and sulk in the cowshed. On one such evening an angel appeared and asked him why he was in such a bad mood. Caedmon complained that he could not sing and the angel said 'Cheer up! Why don't you try to sing just one more time?' So Caedmon tried and suddenly he found he had the most beautiful singing voice and that his head was full of wonderful words to go with it. Caedmon was so excited about this new gift that he rushed to tell Hilda (well, he waited until the morning because Hilda did not like being woken up in the middle of the night). Hilda agreed that he had received a gift from God and she made Caedmon a monk so that he could sing to all the people in the abbey. But if Caedmon tried to sing about ordinary things his croaky, tuneless voice would come back. He could only sing songs to do with God and the Bible. In this picture Caedmon looks as if he has fallen over with the surprise of being visited by a rather stout-looking angel.

St. Cuthbert DIED 687

When Cuthbert was a little boy he was not very interested in being a Christian. All he really cared about was playing games out in the fields with his friends. He had much more energy than the other children and wanted to go on playing even when others were happy to go home for their supper. One day when he was out in the fields a three year old came up to him with a message from God. The three year old had a tantrum and lay on the ground stamping his heels into the ground and crying out, 'God put you on the earth to teach grown ups to be wiser, not to play games with children and it is about time you got on with it.' Cuthbert then went home and became more earnest. He became a monk and lived and taught at Lindisfarne as Aidan had done. Cuthbert did not like sleeping. One night when he stayed up with the shepherds keeping watch over the sheep, he saw the most wonderful vision of angels carrying Aidan's soul to heaven. He was convinced that if he could stay up every night he might see visions like that all the time. One night Cuthbert went down to the sea to pray and he went in until the water was up to his neck. When day break came he waded out of the water and knelt down to pray on the sand. Two sea otters bounded out of the water, stretched themselves out before him, warmed his feet with their breath, and tried to dry him with their fur. You can see these two sea otters in the picture if you look carefully. Once when Cuthbert caught some ravens eating the seeds that he had planted he gave them a telling off and taught them how to pray. To thank him

the ravens brought him a lump of pig's lard as a present. Cuthbert would often show this lard to his visitors and invite them to grease their shoes with it.

Archbishop Theodore DIED 690 AD

Archbishop Theodore set up a school in Canterbury with Hadrian, a bishop from Africa. The school taught all sorts of things including Roman Law, astronomy and arithmetic. Hadrian is said to have been able to work miracles to get boys out of trouble with their teachers.

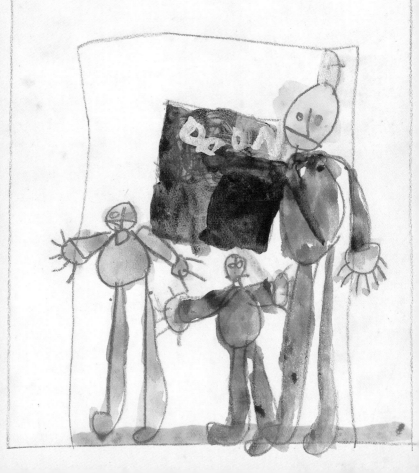

St. Guthlac 673 – 714 AD

Until he was twenty four years old Guthlac worked as a soldier, and a very brave soldier at that. But one day Guthlac had a dream telling him to give up fighting, so he told his fellow soldiers that they must find a new leader. Even the horses looked sad when he announced this news. Guthlac became a monk near Repton. At first the other monks did not like him because he would not get drunk with them. Sometime later he moved to the island of Crowland which could be reached only by boat. He made friends with the wild animals and the fishes from the muddy marshes that surrounded his home. It was said that if he laid a single piece of straw in a basket then a bird would bring more twigs and leaves and build their nest there to please him.

Although Guthlac lived alone on the island, visitors would travel to see him. The birds were not so friendly to the visitors as they were to Guthlac though. A visitor called Wilfrid had his gloves stolen by a jackdaw, and another visitor found that the parchment he was writing on was whisked off his desk and carried away in a bird's beak. But Guthlac prayed for the safe return of these objects and no sooner had he done so than the gloves fell from the sky and the parchment was discovered balanced on a reed in the marshes. It had not got wet and nor had a single letter smudged. Sometimes Guthlac's visitors were not so friendly – indeed some of his visitors were like the kind of thing you meet in nightmares. Demons disguised as beasts would arrive and make his whole house tremble, monsters would burst in to his house from all sides giving poor Guthlac a terrible fright. St. Batholomew solved Guthlac's problem by giving him a scourge to beat the demons with. Guthlac too could perform miracles. Guthlac covered a man with his sheep-skin rug and the thorn that was stuck in the man's foot shot out like an arrow loosed from a bow.

GUTHLAC WAS A WARRIOR ONE NIGHT WEN HE WAS ASLEEP HE SAW HOW NAUGHTY HE WAS! HE GAVE UP HIS FIGHTING AND LIVED ALL ALONE WITH THE BIRDS

THE VENERABLE BEDE

WROTE - 73

A HISTORY

TRANSLATED AND

S.JOHN'S GOSPEL INTO ENGLISH